Fife Council Education Department
King's Road Primary School
King's Crescent, Rosyth KY11 2RS

WHAT IS WEATHER?

Snow

Miranda Ashwell and Andy Owen

First published in Great Britain by Heinemann Library,
Halley Court, Jordan Hill, Oxford OX2 8EJ,
a division of Reed Educational and Professional Publishing Ltd.
Heinemann is a registered trademark of Reed Educational & Professional Publishing Limited.

OXFORD MELBOURNE AUCKLAND
JOHANNESBURG BLANTYRE GABORONE
IBADAN PORTSMOUTH NH (USA) CHICAGO

Designed by David Oakley
Illustrations by Jeff Edwards
Printed and bound in Hong Kong/China

03 02 01 00
10 9 8 7 6 5 4 3 2

ISBN 0 431 03824 4

British Library Cataloguing in Publication Data

Ashwell, Miranda
What is snow?. - (What is weather?)
1. Snow - Juvenile literature
I. Title II. Owen, Andy
551.5'784

ISBN 0431038244

Acknowledgments
The Publishers would like to thank the following for permission to reproduce photographs:
B & C Alexander: pp5, 9, 16, A Hawthorne p22; Bruce Coleman Limited: p13, J Johnson p14, H Reinhard pp6, 20, K Taylor p4, M Taylor p22, S Widstrand pp18, 19; Robert Harding Picture Library: p23, N Blythe p28, L Burridge p7, Explorer p29, J Robinson p26; Oxford Scientific Films: C Monteath p8, B Osborne p15; Pictor International: p11; Planet Earth Pictures: S Nicholls p17; SIPA: Le Progres p27; Still Pictures: T Thomas p12; Tony Stone Images: J Stock p24.

Cover: B & C Alexander, The Stock Market.

Every effort has been made to contact copyright holders of any material reproduced in this book. Any omissions will be rectified in subsequent printings if notice is given to the Publisher.

Any words appearing in the text in bold, **like this**, are explained in the Glossary.

Contents

What is snow?

This **snowflake** is shown 20 times larger than its real size. It was made in a cloud from lots of tiny water drops. The drops were so cold that they turned to ice.

The ice became snowflakes. When snowflakes fall from the sky, we say that it is snowing. On very cold days, snow can cover the ground.

What is frost?

The air is full of tiny water droplets. They can **freeze** on cold nights. The frozen droplets make a thin layer of ice on twigs and branches. This is called **frost**.

On very cold days, rivers and ponds
can be covered with a thin layer of ice.
The ice looks strong, but it will break
where it is thin. You should never
walk on ice.

Snow on mountains

Over high ground the air is cold. Water drops in the clouds **freeze** and fall as snow. Even in hot places, some mountains are always covered in ice and snow.

Over many years the layers of snow are crushed together and turned into ice. The ice flows and slides slowly down the mountain in a **glacier**.

The coldest places

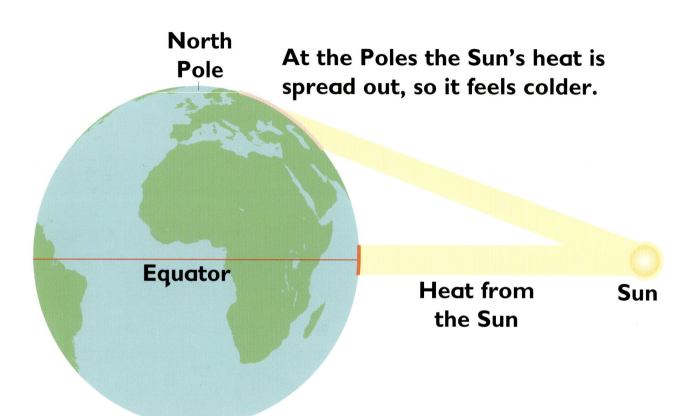

North Pole

At the Poles the Sun's heat is spread out, so it feels colder.

Equator

Heat from the Sun

Sun

The Sun never feels very warm near the North and South Poles. These places are the coldest parts of the world.

Sunlight shining on snow is very bright.
People have to wear sun-glasses as well
as very warm clothes when they are
near the Poles.

The North and South Poles

The South Pole is in **Antarctica**. Here, the land is covered in snow and ice. Penguins huddle together to keep warm.

The North Pole is in the **Arctic**. There is no land here. Much of the sea has frozen into thick ice. Whales and seals swim beneath the ice.

Icebergs

There are huge **glaciers** at the Poles. They move towards the sea. Warmer weather makes the ice melt. Huge chunks of ice break away to become **icebergs**.

Icebergs are mountains of ice that float on the sea. Nearly all of an iceberg is hidden under the water.

Frozen ground

Land close to the Poles is cold. The ground is covered in deep snow. People travel on sledges, skis or snowmobiles like this one.

Land near the Poles is frozen hard.
Only the top layer of the ground **thaws**
during the short summer. The rivers fill
up with water from melted snow.

Animals in the snow

Animals that live in snowy places keep warm by having thick layers of fur. This white wolf cannot be seen easily when she is hunting.

Some animals change colour to help them hide from danger. These hares grow thick, white coats to hide them in the winter snow. In summer their coats are brown.

Plants in the snow

Mountain plants have special ways of growing in cold, snowy places. These flowers have thick, furry petals to keep out the cold.

These trees have special leaves to
protect them from the cold. Snow
slides off easily because the thin
leaves point downwards.

Working in the snow

Snow and ice can **freeze** your fingers and toes. People who work in cold, snowy places wear special clothes to protect them.

The Lapp people live among the
wild reindeer. They use thick,
warm, reindeer skins to make
tents, boots and clothes.

Fun in the snow

The best snowballs are made of wet snow. Wet snow is only just frozen so it makes soft, wet snowballs.

Snow has a smooth surface, so it is easy to slide on. A sledge moves very fast on the slippery snow.

Blizzard!

A snowstorm is called a **blizzard**.
Heavy falls of snow cause problems.
People may be trapped when blizzards
block roads.

Heavy snow and ice can break electric power-lines. Many homes will be without electricity. Without electricity these homes have no light or heat.

Snow accidents

Snow at the top of a mountain can suddenly fall down steep slopes. This is an **avalanche**. It picks up more snow as it sweeps down the side of the mountain.

Avalanches are very dangerous.
These men have rescued someone who
was trapped in fallen snow. They had
to work quickly to find this person.

It's amazing!

Antarctica is the coldest place in the world. The ice in Antarctica is thousands of years old. In some places it is 3000 metres thick.

Snow fell in the Kalahari **Desert** in Africa on 1 September 1981.

Inuit people used to build houses from blocks of snow.

The record for the most snow to fall during a 24-hour period is 190.5 centimetres at Silver Lake, Colorado, USA, on 14 April 1921.

Glossary

Antarctica land at the southernmost part of the world, around the South Pole

Arctic frozen area at the northernmost part of the world, around the North Pole

avalanche a sudden fall of snow down the side of a mountain

blizzard a storm of heavy snow

desert a place that is very dry, and usually very hot

freeze when water turns to ice

frost droplets of water in the air, too small to see, that freeze and turn to ice

glacier a river of ice

iceberg a mountain of ice floating in the sea

Inuit people who live in the coldest parts of North America and Greenland

snowflake a piece of ice that forms a six-sided shape. Snowflakes fall from the clouds when it snows.

thaw a thaw happens when warmer weather makes the snow melt

Index